Buzz! A Honeybee's Quest

BY KIM THOMPSON

A Little Honey Book

Crabtree Publishing
crabtreebooks.com

Tips for Teachers and Caregivers

This book supports early readers as they decode words to learn facts and gain knowledge about the world.

Before reading, make sure students understand the sound-spelling correspondences shown below as well as the high-frequency words shown on the next page. Introduce the vocabulary words.

During reading, provide feedback and encouragement as students sound out decodable words by blending individual sounds.

After reading, talk about and write about the topic. Share the information on page 16 to help students learn more.

Letters and Sounds

New:

Sound	Spelling
/kw/	qu
/z/	z

Review:

Sound	Spelling
short a	a
/b/	b
/k/	c, ck, k
/d/	d
short e	e
/f/	f
/g/	g
/h/	h
short i	i
/j/	j

Sound	Spelling
/l/	l
/m/	m
/n/	n
short o	o
/p/	p
/r/	r
/s/	s
/t/	t
short u	u
/v/	v
/w/	w, wh
/ks/	x
/y/	y

2

Decodable Words

and, but, buzz, can, fill, fuzz, get, helps, in, is, it, legs, lets, not, nuts, on, plants, press, quest, quick, quilt, quit, quiz, sacks, suck, tells, up, whiz, yum, zigzag, zips

High-Frequency Words

New: by, does, other, their, then, things, use

Review: a, do, eat, find, for, good, how, like, live, make, need, of, people, the, they, this, to, we, what, with

Vocabulary Words

dance

fruits

honey

honeybee

nectar

pollen

What helps make good things for people to eat?

It zips by.

It makes a buzz.

honeybee

It is a **honeybee**!

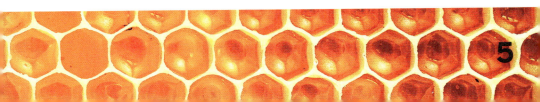

A honeybee is on a quest to find plants. Then, it finds the other honeybees.

dance

It does a zigzag **dance**.

This tells the honeybees how to find the plants.

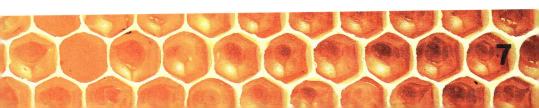

Honeybees whiz to the plants.

They suck up **nectar**.

They get **pollen** on their fuzz.

They fill sacks on their legs with pollen.

Quick honeybees get the pollen to other plants.

This lets the plants make **fruits** and nuts. Yum!

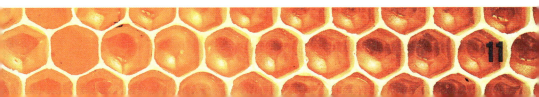

But honeybees do not quit.

They press in like a quilt of honeybees.

They use nectar to make **honey**.

They eat honey to live.

This is a quiz.

What do people need?

Honeybees!

What do honeybees need?

Plants!

People can plant plants with nectar for honeybees.

We can help honeybees get what they need.

Build Background Knowledge

Honeybees are important pollinators, and their populations are in danger. Honeybees pollinate about one-third of the plants that make food for people, including apples, melons, broccoli, almonds, and many more. Bees need flowering plants in their habitats to provide nectar for making honey to eat. Both humans and honeybees change the environment by living and growing. Honeybees change plants in ways that help people survive. How can people make changes that will help honeybees survive?

Buzz! A Honeybee's Quest

Written by: Kim Thompson
Designed by: Rhea Magaro
Series Development: James Earley
Educational Consultant: Marie Lemke, M.Ed.

Photographs: All images from Shutterstock

Crabtree Publishing

crabtreebooks.com   800-387-7650
Copyright © 2025 Crabtree Publishing
All rights reserved. No part of this publication may be reproduced, stored in a retrieval system or be transmitted in any form or by any means, electronic, mechanical, photocopying, recording, or otherwise, without the prior written permission of Crabtree Publishing.

Printed in the USA/062024/CG20240201

Published in Canada
Crabtree Publishing
616 Welland Ave.
St. Catharines, Ontario
L2M 5V6

Published in the United States
Crabtree Publishing
347 Fifth Ave
Suite 1402-145
New York, NY 10016

Library and Archives Canada Cataloguing in Publication
Available at Library and Archives Canada

Library of Congress Cataloging-in-Publication Data
Available at the Library of Congress

Hardcover: 978-1-0398-4436-0
Paperback: 978-1-0398-4517-6
Ebook (pdf): 978-1-0398-4594-7
Epub: 978-1-0398-4664-7
Read-Along: 978-1-0398-4734-7
Audio: 978-1-0398-4804-7